GOD'S
BIG
BOOK OF
VIRTUES

RELATED TITLES PUBLISHED
BY ONEWORLD

God's BIG Instruction Book

Words to Comfort, Words to Heal

GOD'S
BIG
BOOK OF
VIRTUES

A Treasury of Wisdom for
Living a Good Life

COMPILED BY JULIET MABEY

ONEWORLD
OXFORD

GOD'S BIG BOOK OF VIRTUES

Oneworld Publications
(Sales and Editorial)
185 Banbury Road
Oxford OX2 7AR
England
http://www.oneworld-publications.com

Oneworld Publications
(US Marketing Office)
160 N Washington St.
4th floor, Boston
MA 02114

ISBN 1–85168–171–X

Cover and text design by Design Deluxe, Bath
Printed by Graphicom Srl, Vicenza, Italy

CONTENTS

PREFACE

"HAPPINESS," DECLARED Aristotle, "is the meaning and purpose of life, the whole aim and end of human existence." Many things in life can bring us happiness – our friends and family, success in work or study, the beauty of a work of art – yet true, enduring happiness stems from an inner quality, from an understanding and acceptance of the world and our place in it. Without this inner peace and contentment, we can never be truly happy, no matter how much money we have or how successful we are.

But what is this inner peace and how can we achieve it? In spiritual terms, inner peace is often linked to our closeness to God – the closer we are to God, the more at peace we will be. But how can we draw nearer to God? What can we do to progress along the spiritual path, when we spend every day surrounded by the material world?

The spiritual path is not only the path from self to God; it is also the path from selfishness to selflessness. As George Eliot once remarked, "What do we live for, if it is not to make life less difficult for each other?" Virtues represent the practical wisdom we can use to help us – we must put virtues into action in order to progress along the spiritual path. If we renounce our "Me-centered" lives and embrace a virtuous life in which we strive to do only those things we know in our hearts are right, avoiding those actions we know are wrong or harmful, we will not only transform the lives of our fellow human beings, we will also transform our own lives, draw closer to God, and find that inner peace which brings joy to our lives.

The quotations included in this book have been selected to help us cultivate these virtues in our everyday lives. Distilled from both sacred and secular writing, from philosophers, novelists and poets, and from well-known figures of the past whose teachings have stood the test of time to lesser-known writers of today, the selection embraces the values that abide throughout the world, irrespective of race, religion, or culture.

On page 88 of this book, Martin Luther King refers to love of self as the "length" of life; love of others as the "breadth" of life and love of God as the "height" of life. By applying virtues such as those featured in this book, and living lives filled with love, honesty, and self-discipline, we nurture all three of these "life-dimensions" and can have a life that is three-dimensional, complete and blessed with true happiness.

JULIET MABEY

VIRTUE IS a kind of health, beauty, and habit of the soul.

PLATO, *The Republic*

BIRTH DOES not lead to greatness; but the cultivation of virtues by a person leads to greatness.

JAINISM: *Vajjalagam 687*

NO BEAUTY leaves such an impression, strikes so deep, or links the souls of men closer than virtue.

ROBERT BURTON, *Anatomy of Melancholy*

THE FIRST step to Virtue is to love Virtue in another.

THOMAS FULLER, *Gnomologia*

A SPIRITUAL LIFE

T REAT PEOPLE in such a way and live amongst them in such a manner that if you die they will weep over you; alive they crave for your company.

ISLAM: *Nahjul Balagha, Saying 9*

DO ALL the good you can
By all the means you can
In all the ways you can
In all the places you can
To all the people you can
As long as ever you can.

JOHN WESLEY

L ORD, MAKE me an instrument of your peace; where there is hatred, let me sow love; where there is injury, pardon; where there is doubt, faith; where there is despair, hope; where there is darkness, light; and where there is sadness, joy.

O Divine Master, grant that I may not so much seek to be consoled as to console; to be understood as to understand; to be loved as to love; for it is in giving that we receive; it is in pardoning that we are pardoned; and it is in dying that we are born to eternal life. Amen.

ST. FRANCIS OF ASSISI

T HEY ASKED a Chinese wise man, "What is science?" He said, "Science is to know people." Then they asked, "And what is virtue?" He answered, "Virtue is to love people."

LEO TOLSTOY, *A Calendar of Wisdom*

MAN MUST acquire heavenly qualities and attain divine attributes. He must become the image and likeness of God. He must seek the bounty of the eternal, become the manifestor of the love of God, the light of guidance, the tree of life, and the depository of the bounties of God. That is to say, man must sacrifice the qualities and attributes of the world of nature for the qualities and attributes of the world of God.

BAHÁ'Í FAITH: *Promulgation of Universal Peace 451*

THE JOY of life is living it and doing things of worth,
In making bright and fruitful all the barren spots of earth.
In facing odds and mastering them and rising from defeat,
And making true what once was false, and what was
  bitter, sweet.
For only he knows perfect joy whose little bit of soil
Is richer ground than what it was when he began to toil.

ANON

If YOU can keep your head when all about you
    Are losing theirs and blaming it on you;
If you can trust yourself when all men doubt you,
    But make allowance for their doubting too;
If you can wait and not be tired by waiting,
    Or, being lied about, don't deal in lies,
Or, being hated, don't give way to hating,
    And yet don't look too good, nor talk too wise;

If you can dream – and not make dreams your master;
    If you can think – and not make thoughts your aim;
If you can meet with triumph and disaster
    And treat those two impostors just the same;
If you can bear to hear the truth you've spoken
    Twisted by knaves to make a trap for fools,
Or watch the things you gave your life to broken,
    And stoop and build 'em up with worn-out tools;

If you can make one heap of all your winnings
    And risk it on one turn of pitch-and-toss,
And lose, and start again at your beginnings
    And never breathe a word about your loss;
If you can force your heart and nerve and sinew
    To serve your turn long after they are gone,
And so hold on when there is nothing in you
    Except the Will which says to them: "Hold on!"

If you can talk with crowds and keep your virtue,
    Or walk with kings – nor lose the common touch;
If neither foes nor loving friends can hurt you;
    If all men count with you, but none too much;
If you can fill the unforgiving minute
    With sixty seconds' worth of distance run –
Yours is the Earth and everything that's in it,
    And – which is more – you'll be a Man, my son!

RUDYARD KIPLING

THE COMPLETE mystic "way" includes both intellectual belief and practical activity; the latter consists in getting rid of the obstacles in the self and in stripping off its base characteristic and vicious morals, so that the heart may attain to freedom from what is not God and to constant recollection of Him.

AL-GHAZZALI, *Deliverance from Error*

IF I can stop one heart from breaking,
I shall not live in vain:
If I can ease one life the aching,
Or cool one pain,
Or help one fainting robin
Unto his nest again,
I shall not live in vain.

EMILY DICKINSON

I WOULD be true, for there are those who trust me;
   I would be pure, for there are those who care;
I would be strong, for there is much to suffer;
   I would be brave, for there is much to dare.
I would be friend of all – the foe, the friendless;
   I would be giving, and forget the gift.
I would be humble, for I know my weakness;
   I would look up – and laugh – and love – and lift.

HOWARD ARNOLD WALTER

ANYONE CAN carry his burden, however hard, until nightfall. Anyone can do his work, however hard, for one day. Anyone can live sweetly, patiently, lovingly, purely, till the sun goes down. And this is all that life really means.

ROBERT LOUIS STEVENSON

B E GENEROUS in prosperity, and thankful in adversity. Be worthy of the trust of thy neighbor, and look upon him with a bright and friendly face. Be a treasure to the poor, an admonisher to the rich, an answerer of the cry of the needy, a preserver of the sanctity of thy pledge. Be fair in thy judgment, and guarded in thy speech. Be unjust to no man, and show all meekness to all men. Be as a lamp unto them that walk in darkness, a joy to the sorrowful, a sea for the thirsty, a haven for the distressed, an upholder and defender of the victim of oppression. Let integrity and uprightness distinguish all thine acts. Be a home for the stranger, a balm to the suffering, a tower of strength for the fugitive. Be eyes to the blind, and a guiding light unto the feet of the erring. Be an ornament to the countenance of truth, a crown to the brow of fidelity, a pillar of the temple of righteousness, a breath of life to the body of mankind, an ensign of the hosts of justice, a luminary above the horizon of virtue, a dew to the soil of the human heart, an ark on the ocean of knowledge, a sun in the heaven of bounty, a gem on the diadem of wisdom, a shining light in the firmament of thy generation, a fruit upon the tree of humility.

BAHÁ'Í FAITH: *Gleanings from the Writings of Bahá'u'lláh 130*

O MAY I join the choir invisible
Of those immortal dead who live again
In minds made better by their presence; live
In pulses stirred to generosity,
In deeds of daring rectitude, in scorn
Of miserable aims that end with self,
In thoughts sublime that pierce the night like stars,
And with their mild persistence urge men's minds
To vaster issues . . .
             May I reach
That purest heaven – be to other souls
The cup of strength in some great agony,
Enkindle generous ardor, feed pure love,
Beget the smiles that have no cruelty,
Be the sweet presence of good diffused,
And in diffusion ever more intense!
So shall I join the choir invisible,
Whose music is the gladness of the world.

GEORGE ELIOT

COMPASSION

BY COMPASSION we make others' misery our own, and so, by relieving them, we relieve ourselves also.

SIR THOMAS BROWNE, *Religio Medici*

COMPASSION IS the chief law of human existence.

FEODOR DOSTOEVSKY, *The Idiot*

WHEN A man has compassion for others, God has compassion for him.

JUDAISM: *Talmud*

O GOOD man! One who acts good is the "true thinking."
The true thinking is compassion.
Compassion is the Tathagata.

O good man! Compassion is the bodhi path;
The bodhi path is the Tathagata.
The Tathagata is compassion.

O good man! Compassion is Great Brahma.
Great Brahma is compassion.
Compassion is the Tathagata.

O good man! Compassion acts as parent to all beings.
The parent is compassion.
Know that compassion is the Tathagata.

O good man! Compassion is the Buddha nature of all beings.
Such a Buddha nature is long overshadowed by illusion.
That is why beings cannot see.
The Buddha nature is Compassion.
Compassion is the Tathagata.

BUDDHISM: *Mahaparinirvana Sutra 259*

OYE beloved of the Lord! The Kingdom of God is founded upon equity and justice, and also upon mercy, compassion, and kindness to every living soul. Strive ye then with all your heart to treat compassionately all humankind.

BAHÁ'Í FAITH: *Selections from the Writings of 'Abdu'l-Bahá 158*

WHO IS incapable of hatred toward any being, also is kind and compassionate, free from selfishness . . . such a devotee of Mine is My beloved.

HINDUISM: *Bhagavad Gita 12.13–14*

RELIEVE PEOPLE in distress as speedily as you must release a fish from a dry rill. Deliver people from danger as quickly as you must free a sparrow from a tight noose. Be compassionate to orphans and relieve widows. Respect the old and help the poor.

TAOISM: *Tract of the Quiet Way*

CONTENTMENT

R ICHES ARE not from abundance of worldly goods, but from a contented mind.

ISLAM: *Ascribed to Muhammad*

Y OU TRAVERSE the world in search of happiness, which is within reach of every man: a contented mind confers it on all.

HORACE

T HE FOUNDATION of content must spring up in a man's own mind; and he who has so little knowledge of human nature as to seek happiness by changing everything but his own disposition, will waste his life in fruitless effort, and multiply the griefs which he purposes to remove.

SAMUEL JOHNSON

O NE OUGHT not to desire the impossible.

LEONARDO DA VINCI

S EEK NOT that everything should be as you wish, but wish for everything to happen as it actually does happen, and you will be serene.

EPICTETUS, *Enchiridon*

G OD GRANT me the serenity to accept the things I cannot change, the courage to change the things I can, and the wisdom to know the difference.

REINHART NIEBUHR, *The Serenity Prayer*

O Son of Spirit! Ask not of Me that which We desire not for thee, then be content with what We have ordained for thy sake, for this is that which profiteth thee, if therewith thou dost content thyself.

BAHÁ'Í FAITH: *Arabic Hidden Words 18*

L ET NOT your mind run on what you lack as much as on what you have already. Of the things you have, select the best; and then reflect how eagerly they would have been sought if you did not have them.

MARCUS AURELIUS

ONLY WHEN we feel that through all our vicissitudes some unfathomable purpose runs, and that by meeting life nobly and courageously we can cooperate in the fulfillment of that purpose, do we find peace.

ALICE HEGAN RICE, *Happiness Road*

DO NOT be anxious about anything, but in everything, by prayer and petition, with thanksgiving, present your requests to God. And the peace of God, which transcends all understanding, will guard your hearts and your minds in Christ Jesus . . . I have learned the secret of being content in any and every situation, whether well-fed or hungry, whether living in plenty or in want.

CHRISTIANITY: *Philippians 4.6–7, 12*

A SERENE spirit accepts pleasure and pain with an even mind, and is unmoved by either. He alone is worthy of immortality.

HINDUISM: *Bhagavad Gita 2.15*

THOUGH THE fig tree does not blossom,
    nor fruit be on the vines,
the produce of the olive fail,
    and the fields yield no food,
the flock be cut off from the fold,
    and there be no herd in the stalls,
yet I will rejoice in the Lord,
    I will exult in the God of my salvation.

JUDAISM: *Habakkuk 3.17–18*

COURAGE

C OURAGE IS not simply *one* of the virtues, but the form of every virtue at the testing point, which means at the point of highest reality.

C. S. LEWIS

W ITH COURAGE, you will dare to take risks, have the strength to be compassionate and the wisdom to be humble. Courage is the foundation of integrity.

KESHAVAN NAIR

C OURAGE IS rightly esteemed the first of human qualities, because . . . it is the quality which guarantees all others.

WINSTON S. CHURCHILL

H AVE COURAGE for the great sorrows of life and patience for the small ones; and when you have laboriously accomplished your daily task, go to sleep in peace. God is awake.

VICTOR HUGO

P ERFECT VALOR is to do without witness what one would do before all the world.

LA ROCHEFOUCAULD

T HE MASTER said: "To see what is right and not do it, is want of courage."

CONFUCIANISM: *Analects*

I T TAKES a brave man to look into the mirror of his own soul to see written there the disfigurements caused by his own misbehavior.

FULTON J. SHEEN, *Ways to Happiness*

COURTESY AND
CONSIDERATION

I F A man be gracious and courteous to strangers, it shows he is a citizen of the world, and that his heart is no island cut off from other lands, but a continent that joins them.

FRANCIS BACON

T HERE IS a difference between justice and consideration in one's relations to one's fellow men. It is the function of justice not to do wrong to one's fellow men; of considerateness, not to wound their feelings.

CICERO, *De Officiis 1, 28*

O NE SHOULD not behave toward others in a way which is disagreeable to oneself. This is the essence of morality. All other activities are due to selfish desire.

HINDUISM: *Mahabharata*

T SEKUNG ASKED, "Is there one word that can serve as a principle of conduct for life?" Confucius replied, "It is the word *shu* – reciprocity: Do not do to others what you do not want them to do to you."

CONFUCIANISM: *Analects 15.23*

Y OU SHALL love your neighbor as yourself.

JUDAISM: *Leviticus 19.18*

O NE WHO takes a pointed stick to poke a baby bird should first try it on himself to feel how it hurts.

AFRICAN TRADITIONAL RELIGION: *Yoruba Proverb (Nigeria)*

T REAT OTHERS as thou wouldst be treated thyself.

SIKHISM: *Adi Granth*

O NE WHO you think should be hit is none else but you. One who you think should be governed is none else but you. One who you think should be tortured is none else but you. One who you think should be enslaved is none else but you. One who you think should be killed is none else but you. A sage is ingenuous and leads his life after comprehending the parity of the killed and the killer. Therefore, neither does he cause violence to others nor does he make others do so.

JAINISM: *Acarangasutra 5.101–2*

BEWARE! BEWARE! Lest ye offend any heart!

Beware! Beware! Lest ye hurt any soul!

Beware! Beware! Lest ye deal unkindly toward any person!

Beware! Beware! Lest ye be the cause of hopelessness to any creature!

Should one become the cause of grief to any one heart, or of despondency to any one soul, it were better to hide oneself in the lowest depths of the earth than to walk upon the earth.

BAHÁ'Í FAITH: *Bahá'u'lláh and the New Era 78*

USE A sweet tongue, courtesy, and gentleness, and thou mayest manage to guide an elephant by a hair.

SA'DI, *Gulistan*

ONE OF the most important phases of maturing is that of growth from self-centering to an understanding relationship to others . . . A person is not mature until he has both an ability and a willingness to see himself as one among others and to do unto those others as he would have them do to him.

H. A. OVERSTREET

UNLESS WE think of others and do something for them, we miss one of the greatest sources of happiness.

RAY LYMAN WILBUR

O PEOPLE of God! I admonish you to observe courtesy, for above all else it is the prince of virtues. Well is it with him who is illumined with the light of courtesy and is attired with the vesture of uprightness. Whoso is endued with courtesy hath indeed attained a sublime station.

BAHÁ'Í FAITH: *Tablets of Bahá'u'lláh 38*

DETACHMENT

THE MAN who, casting off all desires, lives free from attachment; who is free from egoism and from the feeling that this or that is mine, obtains tranquillity.

HINDUISM: *Bhagavad Gita 2.71*

HE THAT knoweth God loveth Him, and he that knoweth the world abstaineth from it.

HASAN AL-BASRI

LET NOTHING disturb thee,
Let nothing affright thee.
All things are passing.
God never changes.
Patience gains all things.
Who has God wants nothing.
God alone suffices.

ST. THERESA OF ÁVILA

E MPTY THE boat of your life, O man; when empty it will
swiftly sail. When empty of passions and harmful
desires you are bound for the land of Nirvana.

BUDDHISM: *Dhammapada 369*

O GOD! Give to Thine enemies whatever Thou hast
assigned to me of this world's goods, and to Thy
friends whatever Thou hast assigned to me in the life
to come: for Thou Thyself art sufficient for me.

RABI'A

D ETACHMENT IS not a denial of life but a denial of death; not a disintegration but the condition of wholeness; not a refusal to love but the determination to love truly, deeply, and fully.

GERALD VANN, *Eve and the Gryphon*

S ET YOUR affection on things above, not on things on the earth.

CHRISTIANITY: *Colossians 3.2*

T HE TRUE seeker hunteth naught but the object of his quest, and the lover hath no desire save union with his beloved. Nor shall the seeker reach his goal unless he sacrifice all things. That is, whatever he hath seen, and heard, and understood, all must he set at naught, that he may enter the realm of the spirit, which is the City of God. Labor is needed, if we are to seek Him; ardor is needed, if we are to drink of the honey of reunion with Him; and if we taste of this cup, we shall cast away the world.

BAHÁ'Í FAITH: *The Seven Valleys 18–19*

FAITH

Nothing in this world is so marvelous as the transformation that a soul undergoes when the light of faith descends upon the light of reason.

W. Bernard Ullathorne, *Endowments of Man*

Faith is not an easy virtue but in the broad world of man's total voyage through time to eternity, faith is not only a gracious companion, but an essential guide.

Theodore M. Hesburgh, *The Way*

F AITH IS verification by the heart; confession by the tongue; action by the limbs.

Sufi Proverb

T HE FAITH of every man accords with his essential nature; man here is made up of faith; as a man's faith is, so is he.

HINDUISM: *Bhagavad Gita 17.3*

I BELIEVE in a faith that you can see; a living, working faith that prompts to action. Faith without works is like a man putting all his money into the foundation of a house; and works without faith is like building a house on sand without any foundation.

D. L. MOODY

YOU CAN keep a faith only as you can keep a plant, by rooting it into your life and making it grow there.

PHILLIPS BROOKS, *Perennials*

FAITH IS not a thing which one "loses," we merely cease to shape our lives by it.

GEORGES BERNANOS, *Diary of a Country Priest*

I DO not seek to understand in order that I may believe, but I believe in order that I may understand.

ANSELM, *Proslogium*

ABU HURAIRA reported God's Messenger as saying, "The believers whose faith is most perfect are those who have the best character."

ISLAM: *Hadith of Abu Dawud and Darimi*

G OD DOES not die on the day when we cease to believe in a personal deity, but we die on the day when our lives cease to be illumined by the steady radiance, renewed daily, of a wonder, the source of which is beyond all reason.

DAG HAMMARSKJÖLD, *Markings*

I NEVER saw a moor,
I never saw the sea;
Yet know I how the heather looks,
And what a wave must be.

I never spoke with God,
Nor visited in heaven;
Yet certain am I of the spot
As if the chart were given.

EMILY DICKINSON

FAITHFULNESS

B E FAITHFUL, even to the point of death, and I will give
you the crown of life.

CHRISTIANITY: *Revelation 2.10*

H EAVEN AND earth contain Me not, but the heart of my
faithful servant contains Me.

ISLAM: *Hadith of Suhrawardi*

I T IS, however, only in fidelity in little things that a true and constant love of God can be distinguished from a passing fervor of spirit.

FRANÇOIS DE LA MOTHE FENELON

W E MUST strive to be more faithful one day at a time in taking time for others, in doing deeds of kindness, in performing the small everyday run of things faithfully. We must see such as our primary responsibility. Then, says Jesus, the big things will also be taken care of. By the faithfulness with which we fulfill the common daily duties, we make the character which we will have to spend in eternity.

JOHN M. DRESCHER, *Spirit Fruit*

O NLY THE person who has faith in himself is able to be faithful to others.

ERICH FROMM, *The Art of Loving*

FAITHFULNESS IS consecration in overalls. It is the steady acceptance and performance of the common duty and immediate task without any reference to personal preferences – because it is there to be done and so is a manifestation of the will of God.

Faithfulness means continuing quietly with the job we have been given, in the situation where we have been placed; not yielding to the restless desire for change. It means tending the lamp quietly for God without wondering how much longer it has got to go on. Steady unsensational driving, taking good care of the car. A lot of the road to heaven has to be taken at thirty miles per hour. It means keeping everything in your charge in good order for love's sake . . .

Faithfulness is the quality of the friend, refusing no test and no trouble, loyal, persevering, not at the mercy of emotional ups and downs or getting tired when things are tiresome. In the interior life of prayer, faithfulness points steadily to God and His purposes, away from self and its preoccupations.

EVELYN UNDERHILL, *The Fruits of the Spirit*

FORGIVENESS AND MERCY

I F YOU want to see the brave, look at those who can forgive. If you want to see the heroic, look at those who can love in return for hatred.

HINDUISM: *Bhagavad Gita 14.24*

B LESSED ARE the merciful, for they will be shown mercy.

CHRISTIANITY: *Matthew 5.7*

A WISE man will make haste to forgive, because he knows the true value of time, and will not suffer it to pass away in unnecessary pain.

SAMUEL JOHNSON, *The Rambler*

W HERE THERE is forgiveness, there is God Himself.

SIKHISM: *Adi Granth*

G OD HAS been very gracious to me, for I never dwell upon anything wrong which a person has done, so as to remember it afterwards. If I do remember it, I always see some other virtue in that person.

ST. THERESA OF ÁVILA

Y OU MUST forgive those who trangress against you before you can look to forgiveness from Above.

JUDAISM: *Talmud*

T HE BEST deed of a great man is to forgive and forget.

ISLAM: *Nahjul Balagha, Saying 201*

F ORGIVENESS IS not an occasional act, it is a permanent attitude.

MARTIN LUTHER KING

D O GOOD to him who has done you an injury.

TAOISM: *Tao Te Ching 63*

I MUST practice unlimited forgiveness because, if I did not, I should be wanting in veracity to myself, for it would be acting as if I myself were not guilty in the same way as the other has been guilty toward me.

ALBERT SCHWEITZER, *Civilization and Ethics*

TEACH ME to feel another's woe,
To hide the fault I see;
That mercy I to others show,
That mercy show to me.

ALEXANDER POPE, *The Universal Prayer*

LIFE APPEARS to me to be too short to be spent in nursing animosity or in registering wrongs.

CHARLOTTE BRONTË

GENEROSITY AND CHARITY

THERE IS no happiness in having or in getting, but only in giving.

HENRY DRUMMOND

THE WISE man does not lay up treasure. The more he gives to others, the more he has for his own.

TAOISM: *The Simple Way*

Y OU GIVE but little when you give of your possessions. It is when you give of yourself that you truly give.

KAHLIL GIBRAN, *The Prophet*

I F BEINGS knew, as I know, the fruit of sharing gifts, they would not enjoy their use without sharing them, nor would the taint of stinginess obsess the heart and stay there.

BUDDHISM: *Itivuttaka 18*

T O GIVE and to be generous are attributes of Mine; well is it with him that adorneth himself with My virtues. The poor in your midst are My trust; guard ye My trust, and be not intent only on your own ease.

BAHÁ'Í FAITH: *Persian Hidden Words 49, 54*

FOR THIS I think charity, to love God for Himself and our neighbor for God.

SIR THOMAS BROWNE, *Religio Medici*

TRUE CHARITY is the desire to be useful to others without thought of recompense.

EMANUEL SWEDENBORG, *Heavenly Arcana*

FREELY YOU have received, freely give.

CHRISTIANITY: *Matthew 10.8*

HE WHO gives alms in secret is greater than Moses.

JUDAISM: *Talmud*

ONLY THOSE rich men are truly wealthy
Who relieve the need of their neighbors.

Tamil Quatrains 170

THERE ARE three kinds of person existing in the world: one is like a drought, one who rains locally, and one who pours down everywhere.

How is a person like a drought? He gives nothing to all alike, not giving food and drink, clothing and vehicle, flowers, scents, and unguents, bed, lodging, and light, neither to recluses and brahmins nor to wretched and needy beggars. In this way, a person is like a drought.

How is a person like a local rainfall? He is a giver to some, but to others he gives not . . . In this way, a person is like a local rainfall.

How does a person rain down everywhere? He gives to all, be they recluses and brahmins or wretched, needy beggars; he is a giver of food and drink, clothing . . . lodging and lights. In this way a person rains down everywhere.

BUDDHISM: *Itivuttaka 65*

GENTLENESS

G ENTLE CHARACTER it is which enables the rope of life to stay unbroken in one's hand.

AFRICAN TRADITIONAL RELIGION: *Yoruba Proverb (Nigeria)*

G ENTLENESS AND goodness are the roots of humanity.

CONFUCIANISM: *Book of Ritual 38.18*

B E SWIFT to hear, slow to speak, slow to wrath.

CHRISTIANITY: *James 1.19*

MEEKNESS IS an attitude toward God which manifests itself in gentleness toward others. It is an attitude of submission and yieldedness to God which results in the harnessing of our strength in godly ways toward our fellow man. It is love which seeks first not its own, but the things of God and others. The meek accept God's will and dealings without sulking, murmuring, rebellion, or resistance.

C. PAUL WILLIS, *Bells and Pomegranates*

Never speak harsh words, for once spoken they may return to you. Angry words cause pain and there may be blows for blows . . . He who utters gentle instructive, true words, who by his speech gives offense to none – him I call a Brahmin.

BUDDHISM: *Dhammapada 133, 408*

A SOFT answer turns away wrath,
but a harsh word stirs up anger.

JUDAISM: *Proverbs 15.1*

GOODNESS

THE SUPREME test of goodness is not in the greater but in the smaller incidents of our character and practice; not what we are when standing in the searchlight of public scrutiny, but when we reach the firelight flicker of our homes; not what we are when some clarion call rings through the air, summoning us to fight for life and liberty, but our attitude when we are called to sentry duty in the gray morning, when the watchfire is burning low. It is impossible to be our best at the supreme moment if character is corroded and eaten into by daily inconsistency, unfaithfulness, and besetting sin.

F. B. MEYER, *Our Daily Walk*

A GOOD word is as a good tree; its root is firm, its branches are in heaven.

ISLAM: *Qur'an 14.24*

G OODNESS IS love in action.

JAMES HAMILTON

G OODNESS IS something so simple; always to live for others, never to seek one's own advantage.

DAG HAMMARSKJÖLD, *Markings*

T HE GLORY of good men is in their conscience and not in the mouths of men.

THOMAS À KEMPIS, *The Imitation of Christ*

L IVE NOT as though there were a thousand years ahead of you. Fate is at your elbow, make yourself good while life and power are still yours.

MARCUS AURELIUS, *Meditations*

R EAL GOODNESS does not attach itself merely to this life – it points to another world. Political or professional reputation cannot last forever, but a conscience void of offense before God and man is an inheritance for eternity.

DANIEL WEBSTER

I N NOTHING do men more nearly approach the gods than in doing good to their fellow men.

CICERO

T O REFRAIN from evil, to cultivate good, to purify one's mind – this is the teaching of the Buddhas.

BUDDHISM: *Dhammapada 183*

A GOOD man is good even when he is asleep; his character, which comprises several other factors in addition to mere habituation, consists in his moral readiness, the wisdom of his judgment, the sensitiveness with which he can project himself where other selves stand, and the firmness he can show in defending a vision of right.

EDMOND CAIN

G OOD DEEDS are the best prayer.

Serbian Proverb

A MAN'S true wealth is the good he does in this world.

ISLAM: *Hadith of Muslim*

H E THAT does good to another does good also to himself, not only in the consequence but in the very act. For the consciousness of well-doing is in itself ample reward.

SENECA

M Y COUNTRY is the world, and my religion is to do good.

TOM PAINE, *The Rights of Man*

O NE OF the purest and most enduring of human pleasures is to be found in the possession of a good name among one's neighbors and acquaintances.

CHARLES W. ELIOT

HONESTY

TRUTH IS the trial of itself,
    And needs no other touch;
And purer than the purest gold,
    Refine it ne'er so much.

It is the life and light of love,
    The sun that ever shineth,
And spirit of that special grace,
    That faith and love defineth.

It is the warrant of the word,
    That yields a scent so sweet,
As gives a power to faith to tread
    All falsehood under feet.

BEN JONSON

I HOPE I shall always possess firmness and virtue enough to maintain what I consider the most enviable of all titles, the character of an "honest man."

GEORGE WASHINGTON

L ET YOUR conduct be marked by truthfulness in word, deed, and thought.

HINDUISM: *Taittiriya Upanishad 1.11.1*

I T IS easy to be honest enough not to be hanged. To be really honest means to subdue one's prepossessions, ideals – stating things fairly, not humoring your argument – doing justice to your enemies . . . making confession whether you can afford it or not; refusing unmerited praise; looking painful truths in the face.

AUBREY DE VERE, *Recollections*

S PEAK THE truth, yield not to anger, give what you can to him who asks: these three steps lead you to the gods.

BUDDHISM: *Dhammapada 224*

T O LOVE truth for truth's sake is the principal part of human perfection in this world, and the seed-plot of all other virtues.

JOHN LOCKE, *Letter to Anthony Collins*

T HEN HAVE done with falsehood and speak the truth to each other, for we belong to one another as parts of one body.

CHRISTIANITY: *Ephesians 4.25*

I F THE sum of all sins were to be weighed in the balance, falsehood would, on its own, countervail them; nay, its evils would even outweigh them and its detriment prove greater. It were better for thee that thou shouldst be a blasphemer and tell the truth than thou shouldst mouth the formulas of faith and yet be a liar.

BAHÁ'Í FAITH: *Compilation on Trustworthiness 2054*

HOPE

O PTIMISM MEANS faith in men, in the human potential; hope means faith in God and in His omnipotence.

CARLOS CARRETTO, *The Desert in the City*

I F YOU do not hope, you will not find what is beyond your hopes.

ST. CLEMENT OF ALEXANDRIA, *Stromateis*

W E MUST accept finite disappointment, but we must never lose infinite hope.

MARTIN LUTHER KING

T HE VIRTUE of hope is an orientation of the soul toward a transformation after which it will be wholly and exclusively love.

SIMONE WEIL, *Letter to a Priest*

H OPE IS the best possession. None are completely wretched but those who are without hope, and few are reduced so low.

WILLIAM HAZLITT, *Characteristics*

G OD IS our hope and strength; a very present help in trouble. Therefore will we not fear, though the earth be moved, and though the hills be carried into the midst of the sea.

Christian Prayer Book, 1662

HOSPITALITY

HOSPITALITY IS not kindness. It is openness to the unknown, trust of what frightens us, the expenditure of self on the unfamiliar, the merging of unlikes. Hospitality binds the world together.

JOAN CHITTISTER, *In a High Spiritual Season*

DO NOT neglect to show hospitality to strangers, for thereby some have entertained angels unawares.

CHRISTIANITY: *Hebrews 13.2*

S EE TO it that whoever enters your house obtains something to eat, however little you may have. Such food will be a source of death to you if you withhold it.

NATIVE AMERICAN RELIGION: *A Winnebago Father's Precepts*

I DO not want my house to be walled in on all sides and my windows to be shut. I want the cultures of all lands to be blown about my house as freely as possible.

MOHANDAS K. GANDHI

L ET HIM who believes in Allah and the Last Day be generous to his neighbor, and let him who believes in Allah and the Last Day be generous to his guest.

ISLAM: *Forty Hadith of an-Nawawi 15*

THE HUSBAND and wife of the house should not turn away any who comes at eating time and asks for food. If food is not available, a place to rest, water for refreshing one's self, a reed mat to lay one's self on, and pleasing words entertaining the guest – these at least never fail in the houses of the good.

HINDUISM: *Apastamba Dharma Sutra 8.2*

HUMILITY

WE COME nearest to the great when we are great in humility.

RABINDRANATH TAGORE

DOST THOU wish to rise? Begin by descending. You plan a tower that shall pierce the clouds? Lay first the foundation on humility.

ST. AUGUSTINE

S EE WHAT you lack and not what you have, for that is the quickest path to humility.

ROBERT LLEWELYN: *The Cloud of Unknowing*

I T IS humility that exalts one and favors him against his friends.

AFRICAN TRADITIONAL RELIGION: *Kipsigis Proverb (Kenya)*

H UMILITY IS the modesty of the soul. It is the antidote to pride.

VOLTAIRE, *Philosophical Dictionary*

A HUMBLE knowledge of thyself is a surer way to God than a deep search after learning.

THOMAS À KEMPIS, *The Imitation of Christ*

HE THAT is down needs fear no fall,
He that is low no pride.
He that is humble ever shall
Have God to be his guide.

JOHN BUNYAN, *The Pilgrim's Progress*

BE HUMBLE and you will remain entire. The sage does not display himself, therefore he shines. He does not approve himself, therefore he is noted. He does not praise himself, therefore he has merit. He does not glory in himself, therefore he excels.

TAOISM: *Tao Te Ching 7*

WHEN A man is content with the testimony of his own conscience, he does not care to shine with the light of another's praise.

ST. BERNARD OF CLAIRVAUX, *Letters*

EVERY HUMAN creature is the servant of God. All have been created and reared by the power and favor of God; all have been blessed with the bounties of the same Sun of divine truth; all have quaffed from the fountain of the infinite mercy of God; and all in His estimation and love are equal as servants. He is beneficent and kind to all. Therefore, no one should glorify himself over another; no one should manifest pride or superiority toward another; no one should look upon another with scorn and contempt; and no one should deprive or oppress a fellow creature. All must be considered as submerged in the ocean of God's mercy. We must associate with all humanity in gentleness and kindliness. We must love all with love of the heart.

BAHÁ'Í FAITH: *Promulgation of Universal Peace 63*

CONFUCIUS SAID, "A gentleman does not grieve that people do not recognize his merits; he grieves at his own incapacities."

CONFUCIANISM: *Analects 14.32*

W HOEVER EXALTS himself by means of words of the Torah, to what is he like? To a carcass flung into the road from which passers-by protect their noses and keep away.

JUDAISM: *Aboth d'Rabbi Nathan*

INTEGRITY

EVERY THOUGHT I have imprisoned in expression I must free by my deeds.

KAHLIL GIBRAN, *Sand and Foam*

TSEKUNG asked about the true gentleman. The Master said, "He does not preach what he practices till he has practiced what he preaches."

CONFUCIANISM: *Analects 2.13*

A s A flower that is lovely and beautiful, but is scentless, even so fruitless is the well-spoken word of one who does not practice it.

BUDDHISM: *Dhammapada 51*

L ET YOUR acts be a guide unto all humankind, for the professions of most men, be they high or low, differ from their conduct. It is through your deeds that ye can distinguish yourselves from others. Through them the brightness of your light can be shed upon the whole earth.

BAHÁ'Í FAITH: *Gleanings from the Writings of Bahá'u'lláh 139*

N EVER ESTEEM anything as of advantage to thee that shall make thee break thy word or lose thy self-respect.

MARCUS AURELIUS

JUSTICE

J USTICE IS truth in action.

BENJAMIN DISRAELI

J USTICE IS of the spirit, not of the outside world.

HILDA CLARK, *Spiritual Experiences of Friends*

T O DO . . . injustice to another is a far greater evil for the doer of the injustice than it is for the victim.

SOCRATES

T HE BEST beloved of all things in My sight is Justice; turn not away therefrom if thou desirest Me, and neglect it not that I may confide in thee. By its aid thou shalt see with thine own eyes and not through the eyes of others, and shalt know of thine own knowledge and not through the knowledge of thy neighbor. Ponder this in thy heart; how it behoveth thee to be. Verily, justice is My gift to thee and the sign of My loving kindness. Set it then before thine eyes.

BAHÁ'Í FAITH: *Arabic Hidden Words 2*

I F A man is at heart just, then in so far is he God; the safety of God, the immortality of God, the majesty of God, do enter in that man with justice.

RALPH WALDO EMERSON

KINDNESS

THE HEART benevolent and kind
The most resembles God.

ROBERT BURNS, *A Winter Night*

I'M GOING your way, so let us go hand in hand. You help me and I'll help you. We shall not be here very long, for soon death, the kind old nurse, will come back and rock us all to sleep. Let us help one another while we may.

WILLIAM MORRIS

I T IS one of the most beautiful compensations of this life that no man can sincerely try to help another without helping himself.

RALPH WALDO EMERSON

HIM I call a Brahmin
Ever true, ever kind.
He never asks what life can give,
But "What can I give life?"

HINDUISM: *Bhagavad Gita 8.3*

THAT BEST portion of a good man's life,
His little, nameless, unremembered acts
Of kindness and of love.

WILLIAM WORDSWORTH, *Lines Composed above Tintern Abbey*

THOSE WHO act kindly in this world will have kindness.

ISLAM: *Qur'an 39.10*

HAVE YOU had a kindness shown?
    Pass it on;
'Twas not given for thee alone,
    Pass it on;
Let it travel down the years,
    Let it wipe another's tears,
'Till in Heaven the dead appears –
    Pass it on.

HENRY BURTON

LOVING KINDNESS is greater than laws; and the charities of life are more than all ceremonies.

JUDAISM: *Talmud*

If you sit down at set of sun
And count the acts that you have done,
    And, counting, find
One self-denying deed, one word
That eased the heart of him who heard,
    One glance most kind
That fell like sunshine where it went –
Then you may count that day well spent.

But if, through all the livelong day,
You've cheered no heart, by yea or nay –
    If, through it all
You've nothing done that you can trace
That brought the sunshine to one face –
    No act most small
That helped some soul and nothing cost –
Then count that day as worse than lost.

GEORGE ELIOT

ALL THE kindness which a man puts out into the world
works on the heart and thoughts of mankind.

ALBERT SCHWEITZER, *Memoirs of Childhood and Youth*

I SHALL pass through this world but once. Any good therefore that I can do, or any kindness that I can show to any human being, let me do it now. Let me not defer nor neglect it, for I shall not pass this way again.

ANON

O YE lovers of God! Be kind to all peoples; care for every person; do all ye can to purify the hearts and minds of men; strive ye to gladden every soul. To every meadow be a shower of grace, to every tree the water of life; be as sweet musk to the sense of humankind, and to the ailing be a fresh, restoring breeze. Be pleasing waters to all those who thirst, a careful guide to all who have lost their way, be father and mother to the orphans; be loving sons and daughters to the old; be an abundant treasure to the poor. Think ye of love and good fellowship as the delights of heaven; think ye of hostility and hatred as the torments of hell.

BAHÁ'Í FAITH: *Selections from the Writings of 'Abdu'l-Bahá 245*

LOVE

LOVE IS the only force capable of transforming an enemy into a friend.

MARTIN LUTHER KING

CONQUER ANGER by love.

BUDDHISM: *Dhammapada 223*

HE WHO is filled with love is filled with God Himself.

ST. AUGUSTINE, *On the Trinity*

To LOVE is to know Me,
My innermost nature,
The truth that I am.

HINDUISM: *Bhagavad Gita 18.55*

"TEACHER, WHICH is the greatest commandment in the law?" Jesus replied, " 'You shall love the Lord your God with all your heart and with all your soul and with all your mind.' This is the first and greatest commandment. And the second is like it, 'You shall love your neighbor as yourself.' On these two commandments depend all the law and the prophets."

CHRISTIANITY: *Matthew 22.36–40*

THERE IS no other God than Truth . . . To see the universal and all-pervading Spirit of Truth face to face one must be able to love the meanest of creation as oneself.

MOHANDAS K. GANDHI, *Autobiography*

I T IS no great thing to get on well with good and docile men, for that is naturally pleasant to all people, and all men gladly have peace with those and most love those who are agreeable. But to live peacefully with evil men and with impertinent men who lack good manners and are illiterate and rub us the wrong way – that is a great grace, and manly deed, and much to be praised, for it cannot be done save through great spiritual strength.

THOMAS À KEMPIS, *The Imitation of Christ*

L IFE IS short and we do not have much time for gladdening the hearts of those who are traveling the dark way with us. Oh, be swift to love! Make haste to be kind!

HENRI F. AMIEL, *Journal*

S HOW LOVE to all creatures and thou wilt be happy; for when thou lovest all things, thou lovest the Lord, for He is all in all.

HINDUISM: *Tulsi Das*

I LOVED thy creation, hence I created thee. Wherefore, do thou love Me, that I may name thy name and fill thy soul with the spirit of life . . .

Love Me, that I may love thee. If thou lovest Me not, My love can in no wise reach thee.

BAHÁ'Í FAITH: Arabic Hidden Words 4–5

HE PRAYETH best who loveth best
All things both great and small;
For the dear God who loveth us,
He made and loveth all.

SAMUEL TAYLOR COLERIDGE

S PREAD LOVE everywhere you go: first of all in your own house. Give love to your children, to your wife or husband, to a next-door neighbor . . . Let no one ever come to you without leaving better and happier. Be the living expression of God's kindness; kindness in your face, kindness in your eyes, kindness in your smile, kindness in your warm greeting.

MOTHER TERESA

W HAT THEN is the conclusion of the matter? Love yourself, if that means rational and healthy self-interest. You are commanded to do that. That is the length of life. Love your neighbor as you love yourself. You are commanded to do that. That is the breadth of life. But never forget that there is a first and even greater commandment: "Love the Lord thy God with all thy heart, and with all thy soul, and with all thy mind." This is the height of life. Only by a painstaking development of all three of these dimensions can you expect to live a complete life.

MARTIN LUTHER KING

B E IN perfect unity. Never become angry with one another. Let your eyes be directed toward the kingdom of truth and not toward the world of creation. Love the creatures for the sake of God and not for themselves. You will never become angry or impatient if you love them for the sake of God. Humanity is not perfect. There are imperfections in every human being, and you will always become unhappy if you look toward the people themselves. But if you look toward God, you will love them and be kind to them, for the world of God is the world of perfection and complete mercy. Therefore, do not look at the shortcomings of anybody; see with the sight of forgiveness. The imperfect eye beholds imperfections. The eye that covers faults looks toward the Creator of souls. He created them, trains and provides for them, endows them with capacity and life, sight and hearing; therefore, they are the signs of His grandeur.

BAHÁ'Í FAITH: *Promulgation of Universal Peace 93*

MODERATION

T HE GODLIEST form of self-expression is self-control –
maintaining an even keel through the turbulent sea of
human life.

PAUL CROUCH

A MAN should endeavor to be as pliant as a reed, yet hard
as cedar wood.

JUDAISM: *Talmud*

B E GENEROUS but not extravagant, be frugal but not miserly.

ISLAM: *Nahjul Balagha, Saying 32*

H E WHO lives without looking for pleasures, his senses well controlled, moderate in his food, faithful and strong, him . . . [the temptor] will certainly not overthrow, any more than the wind throws down a rock mountain.

BUDDHISM: *Dhammapada 8*

H OW OFTEN has it happened that an individual who was graced with every attribute of humanity and wore the jewel of true understanding, nevertheless followed after his passions until his excellent qualities passed beyond moderation and he was forced into excess . . . A good character is in the sight of God . . . the most excellent and praiseworthy of all things, but always on the condition that its center of emanation should be reason and knowledge, and its base should be true moderation.

Moderation is the silken string running through the pearl chain of all virtues.

JOSEPH HALL, *Christian Moderation*

OBEDIENCE

O BEDIENCE IS the "virtue-making virtue."

GEORGE J. HAVE, *Obedience*

I AM the vessel. The draft is God's. And God is the thirsty one.

DAG HAMMARSKJÖLD, *Markings*

L ORD, MAKE me according to Thy heart.

BROTHER LAWRENCE, *The Practice and Presence of God*

MAKE [GOD'S] will as your will,
so that He may make your will as His will;
make naught your will before His will,
so that He may make naught the will of others
before your will.

JUDAISM: *Mishnah, Abot 2.4*

T O PRAY means to accept and to remember the laws of the limitless being, God, and to measure all your deeds in the past and in the future according to his laws. And it is useful to do this as often as possible.

LEO TOLSTOY, *A Calendar of Wisdom*

S AY: TRUE Liberty consisteth in man's submission unto My commandments . . . Were men to observe that which We have sent down unto them from the Heaven of Revelation, they would, of a certainty, attain unto perfect liberty.

BAHÁ'Í FAITH: *Kitáb-i-Aqdas*

"If ye love Me ye will keep My commandments." (*John* 14.15) If we don't, we shan't. Let no one deceive himself about that. There is no possibility of meeting His claim upon us, unless we truly love Him. So devotion is prior to obedience itself.

ARCHBISHOP WILLIAM TEMPLE, *Readings in St. John's Gospel*

All the things that God would have us do are hard for us to do – remember that – and hence, He oftener commands us than endeavors to persuade. And if we obey God, we must disobey ourselves, wherein the hardness of obeying God consists.

HERMAN MELVILLE, *Moby Dick*

Without commandments obliging us to live after a certain fashion, our existence is that of the "unemployed." This is the terrible spiritual situation in which the best youth of the world finds itself today. By dint of feeling itself free, exempt from restrictions, it feels itself empty.

JOSÉ ORTEGA Y GASSET, *Revolt of the Masses*

T HE TRUE guide of our conduct is no outward authority, but the voice of God, who comes down to dwell in our souls, who knows all our thoughts.

J. E. E. DALBERG-ACTON (LORD ACTON)

O GOD, thou hast endowed conscience with no material force to compel man's reluctant obedience. So give them inwardly a spiritual compulsion in which they will follow it out of choice and delight.

M. KAMEL HUSSEIN, *City of Wrong*

E VERY REVELATION of God is a demand, and the way to knowledge of God is by obedience.

ARCHBISHOP WILLIAM TEMPLE

PATIENCE

PATIENCE AND fortitude conquer all things.

RALPH WALDO EMERSON

PATIENCE MAY be defined as that quality of life which makes suffering creative; and impatience as that whereby suffering becomes a destructive force.

ROBERT LLEWELYN, *A Doorway to Silence*

B E PATIENT under all conditions, and place your whole trust and confidence in God.

BAHÁ'Í FAITH: *Gleanings from the Writings of Bahá'u'lláh 136*

W E GLORY in tribulations also: knowing that tribulation worketh patience; and patience, experience; and experience, hope.

CHRISTIANITY: *Romans 5.3*

B E PATIENT with everyone, but above all be patient with thyself. I mean, do not be disheartened by your imperfections, but instantly set about remedying them – every day begin the task anew.

ST. FRANCIS DE SALES

PATIENCE AND diligence, like faith, remove mountains.

WILLIAM PENN, *Some Fruits of Solitude*

PATIENCE, FORBEARANCE, always win out, not anger. One who is patient becomes established in the Absolute.

HINDUISM: *Mahabharata*

PERSEVERANCE

PERSEVERANCE IS a great element of success. If you only knock long enough and loud enough at the gate, you are sure to wake up somebody.

HENRY WADSWORTH LONGFELLOW

PROSPERITY FORSAKES those who always dream of fate and favors those who persevere. One should therefore always be active and alert.

HINDUISM: Matsya Purana 221.2

C OURAGE AND perseverance have a magical talisman, before which difficulties disappear and obstacles vanish into air.

JOHN QUINCY ADAMS

A LL OUR peace, while we are in this mortal life, rests more in the humble endurance of troubles and of things that are irksome to us than in not feeling them at all. For no man is here without some trouble. Therefore, he who can suffer best will have most peace, and he who is the true conqueror of himself is the true lord of the world, the friend of Christ, and the true inheritor of the kingdom of heaven.

THOMAS À KEMPIS, The Imitation of Christ

O YOU who believe, seek courage in fortitude and prayer, for God is with those who are patient and persevere.

ISLAM: Qur'an 2.153

T HE BEAUTY of the soul shines out when a man bears with composure one heavy mischance after another, not because he does not feel them, but because he is a man of high and heroic temper.

ARISTOTLE, *Nicomachean Ethics*

N O ONE is ever beaten unless he gives up the fight.

W. BERAN WOLFE

P ERHAPS THE most valuable result of all education is the ability to make yourself do the thing you have to do, when it ought to be done, whether you like it or not. It is the first lesson that ought to be learned.

THOMAS H. HUXLEY

A JOURNEY of a thousand miles must begin with a single step.

TAOISM: *The Way of Lao-Tzu*

L IFE AFFORDS no higher pleasure than that of surmounting difficulties, passing from one step of success to another, forming new wishes, and seeing them gratified. He that labors in any great or laudable undertaking has his fatigues first supported by hope, and afterwards rewarded by joy . . .

To strive with difficulties, and to conquer them, is the highest human felicity.

SAMUEL JOHNSON

PIETY AND GODLINESS

THE COMMON element in all expressions of piety, howsoever diverse . . . is this: the consciousness of being absolutely dependent, or, which is the same thing, of being in relation with God.

FRIEDRICH SCHLEIERMACHER, *The Christian Faith*

PIETY IS not an end, but a means: a means of attaining the highest culture through the purest tranquillity of soul.

J. W. VON GOETHE

I F IT be Thy pleasure, make me to grow as a tender herb in the meadows of Thy grace, that the gentle winds of Thy will may stir me up and bend me into conformity with Thy pleasure in such wise that my movement and my stillness may be wholly directed by Thee.

BAHÁ'Í FAITH: *Prayers and Meditations of Bahá'u'lláh 150*

I T IS quite possible to listen to God's voice all through the day without interrupting your regular activities in any way. The part of your mind in which truth abides is in constant communication with God, whether you are aware of it or not.

LUCY HAYS: *A Course in Miracles*

MEEKNESS, HUMILITY, and love,
  Did through Thy conduct shine;
O may my whole deportment prove
  A copy, Lord, of Thine.

CARL SANDBURG, *Lincoln's Devotional*

TAKE MY life, and let it be
Consecrated Lord to Thee.
Take my moments and my days,
Let them flow in ceaseless praise.
Take my hands, and let them move
At the impulse of Thy love.
Take my feet and let them be
Swift and beautiful for Thee.

Take my voice, and let me sing
Always, only, for my King.
Take my lips, and let them be
Filled with messages from Thee.
Take my silver and my gold;
Not a mite would I withhold.
Take my intellect, and use
Every power as Thou shalt choose.

Take my will, and make it Thine;
It shall be no longer mine.
Take my heart, it is Thine own;
It shall be Thy royal throne.
Take my love, my Lord, I pour
At Thy feet its treasure store.
Take myself, and I will be
Ever, only, all for Thee.

FRANCES R. HARVERGAL

C LEANSE THOU the rheum from out thine head and breathe the breath of God instead.

JALALU'L-DIN RUMI

A SPIRITUAL life is simply a life in which all that we do comes from the center, where we are anchored in God.

EVELYN UNDERHILL, *The Spiritual Life*

G IVE ME grace ever to desire and to will what is most acceptable to thee and most pleasing in thy sight.

THOMAS À KEMPIS, *The Imitation of Christ*

C ONSCIENCE IS God's presence in man.

EMANUEL SWEDENBORG, *Heavenly Arcana*

T HE GREATEST attainment in the world of humanity is nearness to God. Every lasting glory, honor, grace, and beauty which comes to man comes through nearness to God. All the Prophets and apostles longed and prayed for nearness to the Creator . . . Nearness to God is possible through devotion to Him, through entrance into the Kingdom and service to humanity; it is attained by unity with mankind and through loving-kindness to all; it is dependent upon investigation of truth, acquisition of praiseworthy virtues, service in the cause of universal peace and personal sanctification. In a word, nearness to God necessitates sacrifice of self, severance and the giving up of all to Him. Nearness is likeness.

BAHÁ'Í FAITH: *Promulgation of Universal Peace 147–8*

V ISIBLE WORSHIP is not condemned, but God is pleased only by invisible piety.

DESIDERIUS ERASMUS, *Enchiridion*

I T IS when you persistently, selflessly perform every action with love-inspired thoughts of God that He will come to you . . . If you are constantly thinking that He is walking through your feet, working through your hands, accomplishing through your will, you will know Him.

PARAMAHANSA YOGANANDA

PURITY

NOT BY sacred water is one pure, although
  many folk bathe in it.
In whom is truth and dhamma, he is pure; he is a
  Brahmin.

BUDDHISM: *Udana 6*

O SON of Spirit! My first counsel is this: Possess a pure, kindly, and radiant heart, that thine may be a sovereignty ancient, imperishable, and everlasting.

BAHÁ'Í FAITH: *Arabic Hidden Words 1*

L ET A man strive to purify his thoughts. What a man thinketh, that is he; this is the eternal mystery. Dwelling within his Self with thoughts serene, he will obtain imperishable happiness. Man becomes that of which he thinks.

HINDUISM: *Upanishads*

P URITY IS for man, next to life, the greatest good, that purity that is procured by the law of Mazda to him who cleanses his own self with good thoughts, words, and deeds.

ZOROASTRIANISM: *Zend-Avesta*

P URITY OF soul cannot be lost without consent.

ST. AUGUSTINE, *On Lying*

THERE IS a polish for everything that becomes rusty, and the polish for the heart is the remembrance of God.

ISLAM: *Hadith of Tirmidhi*

ABIDE PURE amidst the impurities of the world; thus shalt thou find the way of religion.

SIKHISM: *Guru Nanak*

PURITY IS not innocence; it is much more. Purity is the outcome of sustained spiritual sympathy with God. We have to grow in purity. The life with God may be right, and the inner purity remain unsullied, and yet every now and again the bloom on the outside may be sullied. God does not shield us from this possibility, because in this way we realize the necessity of maintaining the vision by personal purity. If the spiritual bloom of our life with God is getting impaired in the tiniest degree, we must leave off everything and get it put right. Remember that vision depends on character – the pure in heart see God.

OSWALD CHAMBERS, *My Utmost for His Highest*

P URITY IS the sum of all loveliness, as whiteness is the sum of all colors.

FRANCIS THOMPSON

T HE MORE pure and sanctified the heart of man becomes, the nearer it draws to God, and the light of the Sun of Reality is revealed within it. This light sets hearts aglow with the fire of the love of God, opens in them the doors of knowledge and unseals the divine mysteries so that spiritual discoveries are made possible.

BAHÁ'Í FAITH: Promulgation of Universal Peace 148

T HE PURE and impure stand and fall by their own deeds; no one can purify another.

BUDDHISM: Dhammapada 9.126

RESPECT

WITHOUT FEELINGS of respect, what is there to distinguish men from beasts?

CONFUCANISM: *Analects*

YOU SHALL rise up before the hoary head, and honor the face of an old man, and you shall fear God: I am the Lord.

JUDAISM: *Leviticus 19.32*

F OR ONE who frequently honors and respects elders, four things increase: age, beauty, bliss, and strength.

BUDDHISM: *Dhammapada 109*

T OLERANCE IMPLIES a respect for another person, not because he is wrong or even because he is right, but because he is human.

JOHN COGLEY

RESPONSIBILITY

T HE PECULIAR character of an individual human being in distinction from an atom lies in this, that he is the owner of himself and responsible to himself.

MARTIN C. D'ARCY, *God and the Supernatural*

O UTSIDE THE sphere of individual responsibility there is neither goodness or badness . . . Only where we ourselves are responsible for our own interests and are free to sacrifice them has our decision moral value.

FRIEDRICH A. HAYEK, *The Road to Serfdom*

O NESELF, INDEED, is one's savior, for what other savior could there be? With oneself well controlled one obtains a savior difficult to find.

BUDDHISM: *Dhammapada 160*

M Y LIFE is an influence on every life mine touches. Whether I realize it or not, I am responsible and accountable for that influence.

RON BARON

M AN IS not intended to see through the eyes of another, hear through another's ears nor comprehend with another's brain. Each human creature has individual endowment, power and responsibility in the creative plan of God. Therefore, depend upon your own reason and judgment.

BAHÁ'Í FAITH: *Promulgation of Universal Peace 293*

E VERY ONE to whom much is given, of him will much be required.

CHRISTIANITY: *Luke 12.48*

S O LONG as men and women believed themselves to be responsible beings, called to choose, and accountable to God for their choices, life might be tragic, but it was not trivial.

SYDNEY CAVE, *The Christian Way*

O YE who believe! You have charge over your own souls.

ISLAM: *Qur'an 5.105*

REVERENCE

DOES NOT every true man feel that he is made higher by doing reverence to what is really above him.

THOMAS CARLYLE, *On Heroes, Hero-Worship and the Heroic*

BE AWARE of Me always, adore Me, make every act an offering to Me, and you shall come to Me; this I promise, for your are dear to Me.

HINDUISM: *Bhagavad Gita 18.65*

F OLLOW AND worship God in the exercise of virtue, for this way of worshipping God is the most holy.

FLAVIUS JOSEPHUS, *Against Apion*

W ORSHIP IS the free offering of ourselves to God; ever renewed, because ever imperfect. It expresses the consciousness that we are His by right, yet we have not duly passed into His hand.

JAMES MARTINEAU, *Hours of Thought*

Worship is transcendent wonder.

THOMAS CARLYLE, *On Heroes, Hero-Worship and the Heroic*

THE SIMPLEST person, who in his integrity worships God, becomes God.

RALPH WALDO EMERSON, *Essays*

IF I worship thee for fear of hell, then burn me in hell. And if I worship thee for hope of heaven, exclude me thence.

But if I worship thee for thine own sake, withhold not from me thine eternal beauty.

RABI'A

RIGHTEOUSNESS

I LIKE life, and I also like righteousness. If I cannot keep the two together, I will let life go and choose righteousness.

MENG-TSE

L ET NOT the nation count wealth as wealth; let it count righteousness as wealth.

CONFUCIANISM: *Great Learning*

I N A region bright with golden luster – center of light and immortality – the righteous after death shall dwell in bliss.

HINDUISM: *Mahabharata*

S O LET us not grow weary in doing what is right, for we will reap at harvest time, if we do not give up. So then, whenever we have an opportunity, let us work for the good of all.

CHRISTIANITY: *Galatians 6.9–10*

C LOTHE THYSELF with the essence of righteousness, and let thine heart be afraid of none except God.

BAHÁ'Í FAITH: *Gleanings from the Writings of Bahá'u'lláh 323*

R IGHTEOUSNESS IS one thing, self-righteousness is another. May God keep me from ever confusing them.

RABBI LIONEL BLUE: Kitchen Blues

THROUGH THE best righteousness,
Through the highest righteousness,
May we catch sight of Thee,
May we approach Thee,
May we be in perfect friendship with Thee.

ZOROASTRIANISM: Yasna 60.21

SELF-DISCIPLINE

DISCIPLINE, TO be sure, is never pleasant; at times it seems painful, but afterwards those who have been trained by it reap the harvest of a peaceful and upright life.

CHRISTIANITY: *Hebrews 12.11*

BRING THYSELF to account each day ere thou art summoned to a reckoning; for death, unheralded, shall come upon thee and thou shalt be called to give account for thy deeds.

BAHÁ'Í FAITH: *Arabic Hidden Words 31*

By degrees, little by little, from time to time, a wise person should remove his own impurities as a smith removes the dross from silver.

BUDDHISM: *Dhammapada 239*

Withdraw into yourself and look. And if you do not find yourself beautiful as yet, do as does the creator of a statue that is to be made beautiful; he cuts away here, he smooths there, he makes this line lighter, this other purer, until he has shown a beautiful face upon his statue. So do you also; cut away all that is excessive, straighten all that is crooked, bring light to all that is shadowed, labor to make all glow with beauty, and do not cease chiseling your statue until there shall shine out on you the godlike splendor of virtue, until you shall see the final goodness surely established in the stainless shrine.

PLOTINUS

Happy is the person who finds fault with himself instead of finding fault with others.

ISLAM: *Hadith*

ONSCIENCE IS a man's compass, and though the needle sometimes deviates, though one perceives irregularities in directing one's course by it, still one must try to follow its direction.

VINCENT VAN GOGH, Dear Theo

HAVE A certain divine sign from God . . . I have had it from childhood: it is a kind of voice which, whenever I hear it, always turns me back from something which I was going to do.

PLATO, Apology

ACH OF you should examine your own conduct, and then he can measure his achievement by comparing himself to himself and not with anyone else; for everyone has his own burden to bear.

CHRISTIANITY: Galatians 6.4–5

O NE IMPORTANT direction in which to exercise gentleness is with respect to ourselves, never growing irritated with one's self or one's imperfections; for although it is but reasonable that we should be displeased and grieved at our own faults, yet ought we to guard against a bitter, angry, or peevish feeling about them . . . What we want is a quiet, steady, firm displeasure at our own faults . . . So then, when you have fallen, lift up your heart in quietness, humbling yourself deeply before God by reason of your frailty, without marveling that you fell; there is no cause to marvel because weakness is weak, or infirmity infirm. Heartily lament that you should have offended God, and begin anew to cultivate the lacking grace, with a very deep trust in His mercy, and with a bold, brave heart.

St. Francis de Sales, *Introduction to the Devout Life*

WHAT YOU are must always displease you, if you would attain that which you are not.

ST. AUGUSTINE, Sermons

THERE IS nothing noble in being superior to some other man. The true nobility is in being superior to your previous self.

HINDUISM: A Proverb

THE LIGHT of a good character surpasseth the light of the sun and the radiance thereof. Whoso attaineth unto it is accounted as a jewel among men.

BAHÁ'Í FAITH: Tablets of Bahá'u'lláh 36

I F ANYONE can control his tongue, it proves that he has perfect control over himself in every other way. We can make a large horse turn around and go wherever we want by means of a small bit in his mouth. And a tiny rudder makes a huge ship turn wherever the pilot wants it to go, even though the winds are strong.

So also the tongue is a small thing, but what enormous damage it can do. A great forest can be set on fire by one tiny spark. And the tongue is a flame of fire. It is full of wickedness and poisons every part of the body. And the tongue is set on fire by hell itself, and can turn our whole lives into a blazing flame of destruction and disaster.

CHRISTIANITY: *James 3.2–6*

SELF-SACRIFICE

T HERE IS but one Virtue – the eternal sacrifice of self.

GEORGE SAND

S ELF IS the only prison that can ever bind the soul.

HENRY VAN DYKE, *The Prison and the Angel*

M AN CAN become part of God's unity, which is eternal, only by forgetfulness of self.

RABBI NACHMAN OF BRATISLAVA

I T IS not only physical bravery that counts. One must have the courage to face life as it is, to go through sorrows, and always sacrifice oneself for the sake of others.

AFRICAN TRADITIONAL RELIGION: Kipsigis Saying (Kenya)

J ESUS TOLD his disciples, "If any man would come after me, let him deny himself and take up his cross and follow me. For whoever would save his life will lose it, and whoever loses his life for my sake will find it."

CHRISTIANITY: Matthew 16.24–25

T HOUGH ONE should conquer a million men on the battlefield, yet he, indeed, is the noblest victor who has conquered himself.

BUDDHISM: Dhammapada 103–5

W HERE RELIGION goes wrong it is because, in one form or another, men have made the mistake of trying to turn to God without turning away from self.

AELRED GRAHAM, *Christian Thought and Action*

O SON of Man! If thou lovest Me, turn away from thyself; and if thou seekest My pleasure, regard not thine own; that thou mayest die in Me and I may eternally live in thee . . .

O My Servant! Free thyself from the fetters of this world, and loose thy soul from the prison of self. Seize thy chance, for it will come to thee no more.

BAHÁ'Í FAITH: *Arabic Hidden Words 7*
Persian Hidden Words 40

A MAN of humanity is one who, in seeking to establish himself, finds a foothold for others and who, desiring attainment for himself, helps others to attain.

CONFUCIANISM: *Analects*

IF YOU could get rid
Of yourself just once,
The secret of secrets
Would open to you.
The face of the unknown,
Hidden beyond the universe
Would appear on the
Mirror of your perception.

JALALU'L-DIN RUMI

L ORD, ENFOLD me in the depths of your heart; and there, hold me, refine, purge, and set me on fire, raise me aloft, until my own self knows utter annihilation.

PIERRE TEILHARD DE CHARDIN

T HEY ARE forever free who renounce all selfish desires and break away from the ego-cage of "I," "me," and "mine" to be united with the Lord. Attain to this, and pass from death to immortality.

HINDUISM: *Bhagavad Gita 2.71*

SERVICE

S ERVICE IS the rent each of us pays for living – the very purpose of life and not something you do in your spare time or after you have reached your personal goals.

MARIAN WRIGHT EDELMAN

O NE DAY a man asked a sheikh how to reach God. "The ways to God," the sheikh replied, "are as many as there are created beings. But the shortest and easiest is to serve others, not to harm others, and to make others happy."

ABU SA'ID

S TRIVE CONSTANTLY to serve the welfare of the world; by devotion to selfless work one attains the supreme goal in life. Do your work with the welfare of others always in mind. It was by such work that Janaka attained perfection; others, too, have followed this path.

HINDUISM: *Bhagavad Gita 3.18–20*

B EAR ONE another's burdens, and so fulfill the law of Christ.

CHRISTIANITY: *Galatians 6.2*

M AN CANNOT live by bread alone. The making of money, the accumulation of material power, is not all there is to living. Life is something more than these, and the man who misses this truth misses the greatest joy and satisfaction that can come into his life – service for others.

EDWARD BOK

D OING GOOD to others is not a duty. It is a joy, for it increases your own health and happiness.

ZOROASTRIANISM: *Zoroaster*

A LL EFFORT and exertion put forth by man from the fulness of his heart is worship, if it is prompted by the highest motives and the will to do service to humanity. This is worship: to serve mankind and to minister to the needs of the people. Service is prayer.

BAHÁ'Í FAITH: *Paris Talks 177*

T HE BEST of men are those who are useful to others.

ISLAM: *Hadith of Bukhari*

WHEN YOU leave this world, material riches will be left behind; but every good that you have done will go with you.

Life should be chiefly service. Without that ideal, the intelligence that God has given you is not reaching out toward its goal. When in service you forget the little self, you will feel the big Self of Spirit.

PARAMAHANSA YOGANANDA

SINCERITY

A MAN becomes pure through sincerity of intellect; thereupon, in meditation, he beholds Him who is without parts.

HINDUISM: *Mundaka Upanishad 3.18*

S INCERITY IS the way to Heaven.

MENG-TSE

I DO not see how a man without sincerity can be good for anything. How can a cart or carriage be made to go without yoke or crossbar?

CONFUCIANISM

THE KINDLING power of our words must not come from outward show but from within, not from oratory but straight from the heart.

ST. FRANCIS DE SALES, *Conferences*

BY THE Truth I mean purity and sincerity in their highest degree. He who lacks purity and sincerity cannot move others . . . True sadness need make no sound to awaken grief; true anger need not show itself to arouse awe; true affection need not smile to create harmony. When a man has the Truth within himself, his spirit may move among external things. That is why the Truth is to be prized!

TAOISM: *Chuang-Tzu 31*

T HE TRULY upright is that which flows out of your genuine innermost self as a result of the sincerity shown by the *kami*; on all occasions, you must exert this sincerity to the utmost, even in the most minor of your activities. Courtesy and ritual without this sincerity and honesty are mistaken and insufficient. It is like drawing a bow and merely releasing the string blindly without firming your hand, or like trying to move in a boat without an oar.

SHINTOISM: *Records of the Divine Wind*

TOLERANCE

B EAR WITH each other and forgive whatever grievances you may have against one another. Forgive as the Lord forgave you.

CHRISTIANITY: *Colossians 3.13*

G IVE TO every other human being every right that you claim yourself.

ROBERT G. INGERSOLL, *Limitations of Toleration*

WHO IS tolerant to the intolerant, peaceful to the violent, free from greed with the greedy – him I call a Brahmin.

BUDDHISM: *Dhammapada 406*

THE LONGER I live, the larger allowances I make for human infirmities.

JOHN WESLEY, *Letter to Samuel Furley*

TO BE silent concerning the faults of others, to pray for them, and to help them, through kindness, to correct their faults.

To look always at the good and not at the bad. If a man has ten good qualities and one bad one, to look at the ten and forget the one; and if a man has ten bad qualities and one good one, to look at the one and forget the ten.

Never to allow ourselves to speak one unkind word about another, even though that other be our enemy.

BAHÁ'Í FAITH: *Bahá'u'lláh and the New Era 80*

L IKE THE bee gathering honey from different flowers, the wise man accepts the essence of different scriptures and sees only the good in all religions.

HINDUISM: *Srimad Bhagavatam*

L ET YOURSELVES be divested of prejudice. If you are good scholars, you learn to treat your neighbors as they should be treated, and to have the same affections for a person from Ireland or England as you do for one from your own native land.

BRIGHAM YOUNG

J UDGE NOT, that ye be not judged.

CHRISTIANITY: *Matthew 7.1*

TRUST IN GOD

T O COMPLETELY trust in God is to be like a child who knows deeply that even if he does not call for the mother, the mother is totally aware of his condition and is looking after him.

AL-GHAZZALI

D O NOT look forward to the changes and chances of this life in fear; rather look to them with full hope that, as they arise, God, whose you are, will deliver you out of them. He has kept you hitherto – do you but hold fast to his dear hand and he will lead you safely through all things; and, when you cannot stand, he will bear you in his arms.

ST. FRANCIS DE SALES

HERE IN the maddening maze of things,
When tossed by storm and flood,
To one fixed ground my spirit clings,
I know that God is good.

I know not what the future hath
Of marvel or surprise,
Assured alone that life and death,
His mercy underlies.

I know not where his islands lift
Their fronded palms in air,
I only know I cannot drift
Beyond His love and care.

JOHN GREENLEAF WHITTIER

THE WINDS of God's grace are always blowing; it is for us to raise our sails.

HINDUISM: *Ascribed to Ramakrishna*

O THOU who art turning thy face toward God! Close thine eyes to all things else, and open them to the realm of the All-Glorious. Ask whatsoever thou wishest of Him alone; seek whatsoever thou seekest from Him alone. With a look he granteth a hundred thousand hopes, with a glance He healeth a hundred thousand incurable ills, with a nod He layeth balm on every wound, with a glimpse He freeth the hearts from the shackles of grief. He doeth as He doeth, and what recourse have we? He carrieth out His will, He ordaineth what He pleaseth. Then better for thee to bow down thy head in submission, and put thy trust in the All-Merciful Lord.

BAHÁ'Í FAITH: *Selections from the Writings of 'Abdu'l-Bahá 51*

N OTHING CAN befall us but what God hath destined for us.

ISLAM: *Qur'an 9.51*

A SK, AND it shall be given you; seek, and ye shall find; knock, and it shall be opened unto you.

CHRISTIANITY: *Matthew 7.7*

SOMETIMES WHEN I was a child my mother or father would say, "Shut your eyes and hold out your hand." That was the promise of some lovely surprise. I trusted them, so I shut my eyes instantly and held out my hand. Whatever they were going to give me I was ready to take. So it should be in our trust of our heavenly Father. Faith is the willingness to receive whatever He wants to give, or the willingness not to have what He does not want to give.

ELIZABETH ELLIOT, *A Lamp for My Feet*

THE LORD is my shepherd. I shall not want.
He makes me to lie down in green pastures;
He leads me beside the still waters.
He restores my soul;
He leads me in the paths of righteousness for His name's sake.
Yea, though I walk through the valley of the shadow of death,
I will fear no evil; for You are with me; Your rod and Your staff, they comfort me.
You prepare a table before me in the presence of my enemies;
You anoint my head with oil; My cup runs over.
Surely goodness and mercy shall follow me all the days of my life; and I will dwell in the house of the Lord forever.

JUDAISM: *Psalm 23*

TRUSTWORTHINESS

TRUST THAT man in nothing who has not a conscience in everything.

LAURENCE STERNE, *Tristram Shandy*

WHEN A man vows a vow to the Lord, or swears an oath to bind himself by a pledge, he shall not break his word; he shall do according to all that proceeds from his mouth.

JUDAISM: *Numbers 30.2*

NEVER ESTEEM anything of advantage to you that will make you break your word or lose your self-respect.

MARCUS AURELIUS

FULFILL THE covenant of God once you have pledged it, and do not break any oaths once they have been sworn to. You have set up God as a Guarantee for yourselves; God knows everything you are doing.

ISLAM: *Qur'an 16.91*

TO BE trusted is a greater compliment than to be loved.

GEORGE MACDONALD, *The Marquis of Lossie*

TRUSTWORTHINESS IS the chief means of attracting confirmation and prosperity. We entreat God to make of it a radiant and mercifully showering rain-cloud that shall bring success and blessings to thy affairs.

BAHÁ'Í FAITH: *Compilation on Trustworthiness 2045*

A GOOD name is rather to be chosen than great riches.

JUDAISM: *Proverbs 22.1*

WORK

FOR GROWTH in virtue the important thing is to be silent and work.

ST. JOHN OF THE CROSS

THANK GOD every morning when you get up that you have something to do which must be done, whether you like it or not. Being forced to work, and forced to do your best, will breed in you temperance, self-control, diligence, strength of will, content, and a hundred other virtues which the idle never know.

CHARLES KINGSLEY

Work is worship.

Hinduism: *Virashaiva Proverb*

The Buddhist point of view takes the function of work to be at least three-fold: to give a man a chance to utilize and develop his faculties; to enable him to overcome his ego-centeredness by joining with other people in a common task; and to bring forth the goods and services needed for a becoming existence.

John Carmody, *Holistic Spirituality*

All action must be done in a more and more Godward and finally a God-possessed consciousness; our work must be a sacrifice to the Divine.

Aurobindo, *Synthesis of Yoga*

H E WHO labors as he prays lifts his heart to God with his hands.

ST. BERNARD OF CLAIRVAUX, *Ad Sororem*

W EEPING IS not the answer to poverty; a lazy man who is hungry has no one to blame but himself.

H E WHO wishes to eat the honey which is under the rock should not be unduly worried about the edge of the axe.

T HERE IS no place where one cannot achieve greatness; only the lazy prosper nowhere. There is no place that does not suit me, O divinity!

AFRICAN TRADITIONAL RELIGION: *Yoruba Proverbs (Nigeria)*

I F A man is called to be a street sweeper he should sweep streets even as Michelangelo painted, or Beethoven composed music. He should sweep streets so well that all the host of heaven and earth will pause and say, here lived a great street sweeper who did his job well.

MARTIN LUTHER KING

I F YOU do your work with complete faithfulness . . . you are making as genuine a contribution to the substance of the universal good as is the most brilliant worker whom the world contains.

PHILLIPS BROOKS, *Perennials*

T HOU SHALT ever joy at eventide if you spend the day fruitfully.

THOMAS À KEMPIS, *The Imitation of Christ*

ACKNOWLEDGMENTS

Every effort has been made to trace and acknowledge ownership of copyright. If any required credits have been omitted or any rights overlooked, it is completely unintentional. The publishers will be glad to make suitable arrangements with any copyright holder whom it has not been possible to contact.

• Bernanos, George from *Diary of a Country Priest*, 1937 by permission of Carroll & Graf Publishers, Inc. • Bok, Edward from *The Americanization of Edward Bok*, 1923 by permission of Simon & Schuster • Carmody, John from *Holistic Spirituality*, 1983 by permission of Doubleday • Carretto, Carlo from *The Desert in the City* by permission of Orbis Books (USA) • Chambers, Oswald from *My Utmost for His Highest*, 1935 by permission of Barbour & Co. • Chittister, Joan from *In a High Spiritual Season*, 1995 by permission of Triumph Books • Churchill, Winston. S. from *Great Contemporaries*, 1937 by permission of Curtis Brown Ltd, London, on behalf of the Estate of Sir Winston S. Churchill. Copyright Estate of Sir Winston Churchill 1937 • Cogley, John from *Commonweal*, 1959 by permission of Sheed & Ward (US) • D'Arcy, Martin C. from *God and the Supernatural*, 1920 by permission of Greenwood Publishing Group • Drescher, John M. from *Spirit Fruit*, 1974 by permission of Herald Press, Scottdale, PA 15603, USA • Elliot, Elizabeth from *A Lamp for My Feet*, 1987 by permission of Servant Publications • Fromm, Erich from *The Art of Loving*, 1996 by permission of HarperCollins Publishers, Inc. • Hammarskjöld, Dag from *Choose Life*, 1968 by permission of Random House Inc. • Hammarskjöld, Dag from *Markings*, 1964 by permission of Faber & Faber Ltd and Alfred A. Knopf Inc. • Havergal, Frances R. from *Methodist Hymnal* by permission of Christian Focus Publications Ltd • Hayek, Frederick A. from *The Road to Serfdom*, 1945 by permission of University of Chicago Press • Hays, Lucy from *Course in Miracles, A* by permission of Foundation for Inner Peace • Hesburgh, Theodore M. from *The Way*, 1963 by permission of University of Notre Dame Press • Kipling, Rudyard from *Kipling: Selected Poems*, 1998 by permission of Orion Publishing Group (Pheonix) • Lewis, C. S. from *The Unquiet Grave* (by Cyril Connolly) by permission of Persea Books Inc. • Llewelyn, Robert from *A Doorway to Silence* and *A Cloud of Unknowing* published and copyright 1986 by Darton, Longman and Todd Ltd and used by the permission of the publishers • Meyer, F. B. from *Our Daily Walk* by permission of Christian Focus Publications Ltd • Mother Teresa from by permission of Servant Publications • Nair, Kesharan from *A Higher Standard of Leadership*, 1994 by permission of Berrett-Koehler Publishers • Niebuhr, Reinhart from 'The Serenity Prayer' by permission of Yale University Press • Ortega y Gasset, José from *Revolt of the Masses*, 1930 by permission of W. W. Norton & Company • Overstreet, H. A. from *The Mature Mind*, 1949 by permission of W. W. Norton & Company • Rice, Alice Hegan from *Happiness Road*, 1962 by permission of Amereon Press • Schweitzer, Albert from *Civilization and Ethics*, 1923 by permission of HarperCollins Publishers, Inc. • Schweitzer, Albert from *Memoirs of Childhood and Youth*, 1931 by permission of Macmillan Publishers Ltd • Sheen, Fulton J. from *Ways to Happiness*, 1953 by permission of Liguori Publications • Temple, William from *Reading in St John's Gospel*, 1939 by permission of Macmillan Education Ltd and Morehouse Publishing Co. Copyright © William Temple 1939 • Van Dyke, Henry from 'The Prison and the Angel' by permission of Ariel Press • Vann, Gerald from *Eve and the Gryphon*, copyright © 1946 Blackfriars Publications, 1998 English Province of the Order of Preachers, Sophia Institute Press, Box 5284, Manchester, NH 03108, USA • Weil, Simone from *Letter to a Priest* by permission of Routledge • Wright Edelman, Marian from speech, 12 May 1990 by permission of Howard University Press • Yogananda, Paramahansa from *Where There is Light* (Los Angeles: Self-Realization Fellowship, 1988) • Yogananda, Paramahansa from Self Realization Summer 1983 (Los Angeles: Self-Realization Fellowship, 1983)

INDEX OF AUTHORS

AND SOURCES